PLR CASH

Generate Maximum Income With Private Label Rights Products!

For a limited time, you can sign up for a GOLD Membership in Resell Rights Weekly for only $1!

As a Gold Member of RRW, you'll receive ...

» Instant Access To 1,257+ Hot Selling PLR & RR Products!
» 64 New PLR/RR Products Every Month! (that's 2 per day!)
» 31 new niche sites every month!
» 700+ PLR Articles Every Month!
» Free Professional Hosting!
» Instant Access to over 100,000 PLR Articles!
» Instant Access to the Backlink Builder!
» Instant Access To The Online Marketing University!
» Instant Access To The Members Only Affiliate Program!
» And A Much More!

Just log into your account and click on the "Upgrades" tab at the top. You can log into your account here: http://Resell-Rights-Weekly.com/members/login.php

Haven't signed up for a free account yet?
Click here now: http://Resell-Rights-Weekly.com

Table of Contents

Disclaimer and Legal Notice.. 4
Private Label Rights Content... 5
What Is Private Label Rights?.. 6
Private Label Rights Terms.. 7
Why Private Label Rights Are So Profitable!... 9
Types Of Private Label Rights Content... 9
    Articles 10
    E-Books and Reports 10
    Software 11
    Scripts... 11
Where to Get Products To Resell... 11
Making Your Private Label Content Unique... 11
Branding Your Private Label Rights Content... 12
Strategies For Maximum PLR Profits Revealed...................................... 12
    Viral Marketing 12
    Affiliate Links 13
    Expert Interview.. 13
    Free Audio... 13
    E-Bay 14
    Content For Newsletters... 14
    Mini eCourses... 14
    Article Pack Websites... 15
    Small Reports... 16
    Physical Products... 17
    Master Resell Rights.. 18
    Bum Marketing... 19
    Firesales... 20
Additional Tips About PLR Content.. 25
    Headline 26
    Sales Page 26
    Software With Private Label Rights 28
    Terms And Conditions.. 28
    Joint Venture (JV) 29
    OTO or One Time Offer... 29

Disclaimer and Legal Notice

The information presented herein represents the views of the author as of the date of publication. Because of the rate with which conditions change, the author reserves the rights to alter and update their opinions based on the new conditions. This report is for informational purposes only and the author does not accept any responsibilities for any liabilities resulting from the use of this information. While every attempt has been made to verify the information provided here, the author and his resellers cannot assume any responsibility for errors, or inaccuracies.

No Liability
No formal product support is provided. In no event will the author of this product, or any distributors, be liable to any party for any direct, indirect, punitive, special, incidental, or other consequential damages arising directly or indirectly from the use of this product. This product is provided "as is" and without warranties. Use of this product constitutes acceptance of the "No Liability" policy.

If you do not agree with this policy, you are not permitted to use or distribute this product. Applicable law may not allow the limitation or exclusion of liability or incidental or consequential damages, so the above limitation or exclusion may not apply to you. The liability for damages, regardless of the form of the action, shall not exceed the fee paid for the product.

Warranties
There are NO WARRANTIES express or implied and specifically no warranties regarding FITNESS FOR SPECIFIC PURPOSE or WARRANTY OF MERCHANT ABILITY of this product.

Earnings Disclaimer
The Seller of this product makes no suggestions, implications, warranties, or guarantees that by purchase resale rights products from this website, or that by following or adhering to any program or information featured anywhere inside this web site or elsewhere, that users will make money. Seller is not responsible for any losses or damages resulting from the use of any product, link, information, or opportunity contained within this web site. Users realize any business has potential risk for loss of capital.

Furthermore, any earnings or income statements used within the Sellers website are only examples or estimates of what you could earn. There are absolutely no guarantees that you'll do as well and you must be prepared to accept the risk of doing not as well. In the event that there are any specific income or earnings figures that have been reported within the Seller website, this must not be considered as average earnings. You must be prepared to accept the risk of doing not as well.

Earnings and income results are based on multiple factors. Every individual is different and will achieve different results. We do not know your education, experience; motivation, work ethic, as well as many other factors that may determine or affect the results of how well you may or may not do.

There are absolutely no guarantees that past successes or prior results are any indication of future successes or results. The internet is a rapidly changing environment. What has worked in the past will not necessarily work in the future. Always do your own due diligence before entering into any business or making business decisions.

Private Label Rights Content

With private label rights content, it has become simpler and quicker to sell products online. This way, you don't have to stump your brain trying to figure out what to write. Using private label rights content can lessen the strain of that.

This is especially true if you're not into or can't do some type of structured writing. The important thing is to make sure you modify your content before it becomes a finished product.

With private label rights content, you must broaden your scope of what you have. It's more than just the article content that was purchased. The amount of profit you make will be determined by how your structure the quality of the content when you modify it.

The quantity has nothing to do with how well your products sell using private label content. You can sell 200 copies and if the content isn't up to snuff, then you might be looking at refunds down the line. So the better structured and informative your content is, the more chance you have of maximizing your profits.

Even though a lot of the information that people are looking for can be found for free on the internet, who wants to spend hours upon hours looking for it? They would just rather pay for information that they can receive in a matter of minutes.

They're looking for products they can access in an instant. That's where you come in. You can be the broker for what they're looking for. People are looking for answers to solve their issues. If you have the information they need in a solid, informative way, they'll buy it from you.

Quality content reigns and it is the key to making lucrative profits in the information era. That is what a lot of people who search the internet are looking for: information. They want information and they want it now, not yesterday, not tomorrow, but now.

If you already have information on the subject, that makes it easy for you. If you don't, it can be very time consuming to look up information. That's why it's good to use private label content and you can modify it to your specifications.

When you're selling private label content, you will get more profits for unique content than you would if you were just selling private label rights content. This is because people don't want to be in the bunch where everyone on the planet has the same thing.

The original writer can sell the same private label rights content more than one time. This concept can make their content profitable to purchase. When you create and sell unique content, the person who purchases it from you is now the owner of the content.

You can continue to make lucrative profits with unique content by charging more money for it. This is because the content itself is original and not some rehashed stuff that has been floating from place to place.

What Is Private Label Rights?

Private Label Rights, or PLR, as it is commonly known as, has taken the internet marketing world by storm. This content is becoming extremely popular and useful for those who are looking to create new products and new content.

Private Label Rights is content that can be sold to others. The content can be edited and modified to the purchaser's desires. These types of rights allow you the flexibility to change sentences, paragraphs and whatever else you see fit to change.

There are occasions, however, where the creator has certain limitations on how you can use the Private Label Rights content. You may not necessarily have the flexibility and the freedom that you thought you had to edit. Prior to your purchase, it is to your advantage if you inquire with the seller as to what the terms are. This way, you won't be stuck with something that you can't do much with.

For the most part, Private Label Rights can be used to edit and modify the content to something different than the original. You will either receive the Private Label Rights content in a .doc (document) file, .rtf (rich text file) or a .txt. (text file).

The document and rich text files are usually in Microsoft Word, the text file usually comes from Notepad. You can also put your name as the author, but it's better if it's been changed from the original first. If the content is what you need, it's good for you because you don't have to spend hours upon hours wondering what to write about.

As mentioned before, you will have to change more than just the authorship to make the content your own. Look through it and see how you can make it better to suit you. You may want to change the wording around in some if not all of the paragraphs. You may want to substitute other words for what is already listed. You don't have to use big words that people don't know the meaning of.

At first, you may think why you are doing these modifications and what purpose does it serve. That's the reason you purchased the Private Label Right content, right? So you wouldn't have to change much of anything, if anything at all. Wrong. You are only one of hundreds of people who purchased the same content.

The seller may or may not have a limit on how many can purchase; it would be advantageous if they did. If they sold the same content to no more than, say, 200 or 300 people, then that's not too bad. Even then, you will have to change your content considerably because there will be those buyers who think just because they have Private Label Rights content, they don't have to change anything.

What they fail to realize is that the more people that provide the same exact unchanged content on their websites and other products, the more the search engines will notice and not give credence to it. This is the type of competition you don't want. If you do decide to go ahead with it, not only will you have competition from clones, you will have to lower the price of your content in order to stay competitive with the others. This in essence, lowers the value of the content.

In order to get the best value for your products, you have to stand out from the crowd. In addition to editing and modifying, find places in the content where you think it could use a little more meat in the body. Make the content worth reading and worth selling to others. In addition to the content, you should also change the title, if there is one. It can mean the difference between blah, mediocre or a hitmaker.

There have been many authors who had quality content, but their title or headline is lacking substance. Which sounds better to you, "Tips to Revive Your Marriage" or "10 Tips To Revive Your Marriage Before You End Up In Divorce Court"? The second title will definitely get people to thinking. They'll want to know how to get their marriage on the right track again or suffer the consequences. Titles and/or headlines should provoke thought and stirring.

Private Label Rights Terms

It's good to want to make a profit with private label rights content, and it can be lucrative. However, you must be mindful of the seller's terms of using it. Copyright laws go into effect when content is created.

So when the seller conducts the transaction with private label rights content, read and be aware of what their terms are and adhere to them. If you don't, you can find yourself in a world of trouble.

Take a look at some of the things that sellers decide on when creating terms for private label rights content:

Sell or not to sell?

More times than not, the seller will allow you to sell the private label rights package to others. If they allow you to sell it, it can possibly set up a devaluing process. This is because others may use the private label rights content as is and not bother to modify the contents in order to be unique.

Package or not to package?

It kind of ties in with the selling part. Some people purchase private label rights content and resell it with content that relates to it.

Changing the content

This is practically a given because that's the purpose of selling private label rights content is to make it unique and different from everyone else. That is the way you can maximize your profits with private label rights content. You have to set yourself apart from the "cookie cutter" people that choose not to benefit further.

Give away

This can be a contributor to making the content devalued. Some sellers choose to opt out of this option.

Offered a bonus or not?

Some sellers allow you to offer the private label rights content as a bonus with products that you already have. Other sellers prefer not to do this because it goes into the devaluing issue again. They think that if you do this, it will put a damper on those who try to sell the work.

Paid membership sites

Some sellers don't care to offer private label rights content to this group because they feel it can get in too many hands when they're looking to limit the quantity sold. It can also devalue the content because most people will be too lazy or don't have time to modify the content to make it unique.

Resale and Master Resale Rights

There are some sellers that will allow you to sell the rights to others.

Selling of Private Label Rights

Normally, this is not allowed because this hurts the seller. Unless you specify a price to sell it for, the buyer will try to sell it for a lesser cost so he can make more sales. This cheapens the cost and the seller can lose money.

Auction Sites

This will cause instant devaluing of the content. There are already people who sell private label rights content on auction sites for $.99 and because of that, the value of the content plummets. This being the reason why sellers usually don't allow the selling of private label rights content on sites like eBay, etc.

There are also times when the seller will offer what is called unrestricted private label rights. That doesn't happen a lot, but when it does, that means you're free to distribute or change the private label rights content in any way you choose. Talk about freedom!

So with these terms in mind, you can decide which ones would benefit you the most and provide more profits to your bottom dollar.

Why Private Label Rights Are So Profitable!

Private label rights can be a godsend for the person who is not author or writer-inclined. They just want to purchase material that doesn't require a lot or brainwork. As discussed earlier, you'll have to make some changes to make your product unique. In addition to that, changing the title can give your product an extra boost. You can brand yourself into lucrative profits with private label content by doing this.

You also don't have to pay hundreds of dollars for a ghostwriter, or pay a lot for outsourcing writers. The only exception would probably be if you're creating software or a script. If you're not programmer or script-inclined, you would probably have to pay for someone to change the software or script format for you. If you can find someone that can do this for you at a reasonable price, then you're good to go.

You can check the more popular internet marketing forums to find a reputable person. The more original you are, the better chance you have of your product selling.

Nowadays, people are looking for something not sold by the status quo. They no longer want to purchase "cookie cutter" products that everyone else is selling. If you make yours different, it will be noticed and people will know that you took the time to set yourself apart. This alone will give them a reason to buy from you.

Types Of Private Label Rights Content

There are different types of private label rights content available to use to make a profit. When you think of content, it isn't just buying articles or reports in document or rich text file format. You can also create software and scripts with private label content and make lots of money.

Articles

There is not a shortage of Private Label Rights articles being sold online. You can find them in forums (in the special offers section) and there are websites that cater to selling batches of articles. These articles are usually written by freelancers from freelance writing groups or the seller writes them, if they have time.

You can also find articles on membership sites. This can be a plus and a minus. There are some membership sites that have articles in addition to other products included in the membership. You may or may not want to whole package. If you don't, it's better to find a website where they just sell articles.

The emergence of article membership sites is getting popular. The monthly fees can range from $10 to $97, with the higher prices usually providing the best quality content, along with other perks.

If your budget can't part with a monthly membership, there are sites that offer free private label rights articles. However, some of these articles may need more work than you're willing to put in time for. It's not a bad idea to check them out anyway; you never know what kind of gems you might find.

E-Books and Reports

This is one of the more popular formats for private label rights content. This is because you have the advantage of creating another product or chop up the content into articles. An average e-book is about 30 – 40 pages. Or you can divide the content into small reports. Not everyone likes to or has time to read an entire e-book.

You can also take an e-book with more pages and divide it into three parts. You would make more money selling 20-page small reports for $15 than you would selling a large e-book for $37. Since these would be your creations, you can also offer resell or master resell rights if you wanted to. There's plenty of opportunity to make lots of money with these formats.

Like with articles, there are membership sites that offer e-books with private label rights. These monthly memberships for the most part, are reasonably priced. The only thing about some of these memberships is that you may not know what next month's content will be until that time comes.

It may be content that you may or may not like. You have to decide whether you would want to spend your money every month, taking a chance that you may or may not like the future month's products.

Software

This can be very lucrative and a great money maker. Software with private label rights can make you more money than selling e-books. You can create or have someone create different software programs for you to sell.

Scripts

Scripts is a form of software that is web-based. These can be edited and modified to use how you wish. Most are very easy to use and you can upload them to your website and use in a matter or minutes.

Another form of private label rights is called the public domain. Public domain is material that is published before the year 1923 that has not claimed copyright status. However, you must be mindful that not every single piece of material falls under that rule. You will have to check governmental sources to be sure that the material is indeed public domain.

There are some membership sites you can join that specialize in providing public domain content. Make sure they are properly licensed to do so. The legitimate sites will usually mention information regarding an attorney being involved. So at least you know that you're getting quality content that you can modify any way you wish.

If you're on a budget and can't do the membership thing right away, the Gutenberg site has plenty of public domain material you can use and modify to create products. Even with that, you will still have to check because there is some material that is not allowed to be used until a certain year or it's not in the public domain. Public Domain content is one of the best ways to generate private label rights products and ridiculously profit off of it.

Where to Get Products To Resell

If you are looking for products to resell, there is no need to purchase them one by one. All you need to do is sign up for a free membership in Resell Rights Weekly. You'll get **MUCH MORE** than enough resources to get started immediately. You'll get instant access to over 130 PLR ebooks & other various products. It is like adding a ton of bullets for your gun. Click here for more info: http://www.resell-rights-weekly.com/

Making Your Private Label Content Unique

If you purchase a private label rights package that includes headers, graphics and a sales page, you can change the images to something totally different. As with the articles and e-book content, people don't want a "cookie cutter" product.

They're looking for something original that no one or not many people have. Sometimes the graphics aren't appealing or the colors on them may be blurry. You wouldn't want to put that on your website. People who are looking to buy would not think it was too professional.

You can have your graphics professionally created by an experienced graphics artist. You can shop around on the internet marketing forums. A lot of times, they offer great deals to forum members. They can charge anywhere from $37 on up, depending what you want.

See if you can negotiate a fair price to do the work. If your budget does not allow for that, Adobe Photoshop has a 30-day trial to use their graphics software. It is about the best graphics software available and will provide you will quality graphics that will make your head spin. In addition to the graphics, you should seriously consider changing the copy on the sales pages.

Doing this will help you stand out from the "cookie cutter" sites and people will be more drawn to purchase from you. For the most part, they can probably tell whether or not your site is different than others who are selling the same thing.

You can still change the wording on your copy even if you're not a master copywriter. If your budget doesn't allow for an experienced copywriter, get a good copywriting manual to study. Or, if you need to have a sales page really quick and you're on a budget, do some research on other sales pages that are similar in your niche area and study them.

You may be able to get some ideas from them. One thing you don't want to do if you're doing this is to copy word for word from their sales page. You would surely be in hot water with a copyright infringement lawsuit.

Branding Your Private Label Rights Content

You may want to consider branding your private label rights product if you really want to stand out. Branding is a way of making the product your own with you as the author. There are several ways you can do this:

You can add your name to the title of your product. For instance, Jane Smith's Strategies For Online Profits instead of just Strategies For Online Profits.

You can also add a logo that represents you or your company. You can do this by using graphic software that has logos or you can hire a graphic designer to do this for you.

You can use a specific name, such as the "Wealthy Business" series. Doing it like this will help you to stand out and be noticed.

Strategies For Maximum PLR Profits Revealed

Viral Marketing

Like a virus, viral marketing can be spread to other people, but in a good way. In this case, if you have a list, you can give your list a free copy of a report you wrote using private label rights material. You can also offer free software as a viral marketing tool. The word "free' is one of the most powerful words in the American vocabulary. People are like magnets to things that are advertised as free.

Your list can be encouraged to forward your free products to others in efforts to get more people signed up to your list. When they sign up to your list and see that you have quality information and products, more than likely, they'll want to buy and you'll make more money with your expanded list. It just goes to show that you have to give in order to receive. Don't underestimate the power of this kind of free marketing. It can do wonders for your bank account.

Affiliate Links

With that free report using private label rights, you can strategically insert affiliate links for related products. This way, you can make some money up front if the person clicks on the link and is interested in the product. However, you have to be careful not to place a lot of affiliate links in the report or it will look like your main objective is to get their money before they can digest the information on the report.

This is a turn off and can cost you potential subscribers added to your list. If you do add affiliate links to the report, they should be cloaked so that it won't be so obvious to others that you're trying to sell something. You want to get them interested in the report first before they pull out their wallet. If you do this the right way, you'll have more commissions than you ever thought you could have.

Expert Interview

To add value and profit to your private label rights product, you could include an interview with an expert. Ask questions regarding the niche and see if the person would provide some answers in relation to your product. With the information the interviewer decides to give, it can help you enhance to value and quality of your product.

You can explain that you interviewed someone and they provided information on the subject. Then you can take the interviewer's information and compile it with your private label rights product. This idea, in addition to you modifying the generic private label rights content, can make your content unique and increase profits for you.

Free Audio

Instead of offering them a free e-book, private label rights content can be used to create audios. As with other media, you should modify the content so you can stand out. This is another way to get opt-ins to your newsletter. This free audio would have lots of value because it would be an original, created by you, not something passed down where every Tom, Dick and Harry have given away as a free gift.

As usual, being unique is the key here. When people get this, they'll start to think that since your free audio has value, that everything else you offer will have value also. Therefore, they'll more likely be eager to purchase from you, resulting in more profits. More importantly, the audio is "free" and people pounce on anything that has the word "free" in it.

E-Bay

For the most part, you're not allowed to sell the original private label rights products or articles on E-Bay. This is because the value will shoot down very quickly and then you'll have copy cats who will try to undercut you by offering lower auction prices. What do you do?

Modify and add to the product, including changing the title to something more attention-grabbing.

Use the "About Me" page to your advantage. In that area, add your webpage that has the opt-in form for them to sign up for your newsletter. Or, if you have a similar product, use that webpage in the "About Me" section. Some customers would be interested in purchasing more private label rights products, especially if you've made significant modifications and changes to the information to make it look unique.

Content For Newsletters

Private label rights articles would be just the thing for newsletter content. Of course, you should modify it to your satisfaction and not do a copy and paste scenario. There may be other newsletters similar to yours that are using the "cookie cutter" tactic by not changing the private label rights content.

The more you change, the more your subscribers will see you as an expert. This in turn, can provide more profits for you. Even though the majority of newsletters are created online, there are some that are still created offline and mailed out. As with the online newsletters, you should modify the private label content to be unique.

Mini eCourses

These are lessons that contain information that can be about the product you want to promote or something related to your newsletter. The courses are put in an autoresponder and sent out at whatever date and time you set them for. The courses should give your subscribers a little information about the niche, but just enough to keep them wanting more. In a sense the courses should be incomplete, not providing everything they need to know.

You can do this with existing private label rights articles. You would take the articles and modify them. If the articles are too long, they can be chopped up so that your subscribers would only get a portion every other day or every few days. It's better to spread them out so they will have time to read and digest them.

You have to pick a theme for your course, such as weight loss. You can have an e-course that talks about five effective ways to lose weight safely. You could title it like this: Weight Loss Strategies: Five Exercises That Can Help You Slim Down. The title should be something that will catch your subscribers' eyes.

This is good because it lets your subscribers know that they don't have to use diet pills and other supplements to lose weight. If you don't have any private label rights articles, you can check some of the forums and websites that sell individual PLR article packs. Be sure that your e-course lessons are formatted properly. You should also have an opt-in form along with a brief sales page to sell the e-course.

Even though it is free, you still have to convince people that your e-course has information that they want to know about. They'll want to know what's in it for them; how can your e-course help them?

An e-course will help your subscribers know who you are because they'll be receiving information from you on a consistent basis. So, what does this have to do with profits? When you put forth an effort to initially educate your subscribers in your newsletter, the more chance you have of them purchasing your products.

You have established a relationship with them and not just looking to make a quick buck. You can insert links to your products or affiliate products. A lot of subscribers appreciate that and creating an e-course modified using private label articles will help them as well as help you bring in plenty of profits. You will stand out as an expert in your field.

Article Pack Websites

There are some people who have these set up for the convenience of those who do not want to pay monthly for an article membership site. You can offer private label rights article packs that people would want to purchase. You would probably have to browse through different forums and find out what topics are actively being discussed.

You can also use keyword research to find out what people are looking for and choose categories from your findings. Unless you find someone who sells their private label rights material at a cheap price, most of the article batches will be priced higher than they would if they were in a membership site. You have to pay for convenience.

Even with that, the articles should be of good quality. You can subtlety advertise on different forums and pay per click (PPC) websites, such as Google. People are not going to always have time to create their own articles, so purchasing private label articles from you would be profitable for your bank account, especially if your articles are of good quality.

Small Reports

This was mentioned briefly earlier in the report. Small reports using private label rights are very profitable. For one, modifying the content and even changing the title is crucial to your reports' uniqueness and branding. The reports will show your personal sense of writing style and information. There are other advantages of small reports as well. They are easier to write and you don't have to spend weeks writing 10 – 15 pages.

You can take a bunch of private label articles, modify them and put it together as a report. You may have to add some information in between to give the report some meat, but other than that, you're looking at a solid profit machine if done correctly.

You should select a market based on your target audience. Some of the popular ones to choose from are:

- Online Business
- Parenting
- Weight Loss
- Money and Finance
- Self-improvement
- Weddings
- Health-related issues
- Sports
- Cooking
- Recipes

Before you start creating the reports, find out what your customers want. You can do this by surveying them. You don't want to waste time creating original reports that people don't want. When that is determined, find out what's out there. This way, you'll know whether or not there's too much competition.

In fact, you should study the competition. If your customers want the same type product that's in another market, you have to find a way to make yours unique. Your report must stand out in order for it to sell. You can purchase private label rights content and modify it. You can also add information to it to make it your own and brand yourself.

Some ideas for small reports titles can be:

- 7 Ways To Slim Down In A Matter Of Months
- 5 Ways To Boost Your Self-Esteem And Eliminate the Negativity
- 10 Tips to Save On Your Wedding And Not Be Broke

- How To De-Stress And Have A Content Life
- How To Build An Responsive Mailing List
- How To Remove Acne From Your Facial Area

Small reports are also easier to sell. It's easier for people to purchase small reports at a lesser price than it is to purchase a large e-book at $47. Small reports can be digested in one setting, whereas e-books with a lot of pages take longer to read.

Even if the report is not up to their expectations, they're more likely to keep it than get a refund for $10. For more profits, you can use the small reports and bundle them together at a special price.

For example, you can offer a bundle of five small reports for $37 and counter it with the individual reports for $10. People can decide which would be better for them. Sometimes, they don't want or need all of the reports. However, there are some who will think between the two and go for the bundled value, which in turn can mean more profits for you.

Physical Products

The value and profits in private label rights material is greater when you use them to create physical products. You can modify the content and use it to create CDs and DVDs and printed books. More people prefer audio and video products in addition to the instant downloads. Creating audio is easy. You just need a microphone and you can use Audacity, the free audio software to create your product using the modified private label rights material.

If you don't want to record it yourself, you can hire someone else to do it. Check out the forums for people that offer those services. Ask them for a sample so you can hear how their voice sounds. With audio, you can listen to the material at your leisure, even when you're laying down with your eyes closed.

Or you can transfer the audio to your iPod or mp3 player and listen to it while you're walking, driving or even when you're flying. The fact that audio is mobile makes audio products profitable. You can't do that with an e-book.

You can also use private label material to create video products. There is a version of Camtasia, which is a very popular video software, that you can get for free and it comes with instructions on how to use it. Video is becoming more and more popular nowadays. With video, you can sit down and actually watch what is going on, as opposed to reading it from an e-book.

Some people learn better from looking at instructions from a video than they do an e-book, especially since the procedure is usually shown step-by-step. That's because they're actually looking at the process and can follow along instead of reading it and not being able to picture what's going on. It's also good for those who don't catch on quickly.

They can replay the video over and over until it sticks in their brain. A good idea for this type of media would be workshops and conferences that last for several hours and contain a lot of information. You can also create videos to upload on YouTube to get traffic, but these wouldn't be physical products. Still, uploading them to get traffic to your site is a great idea.

In addition to that, videos created on DVD can be sold on E-Bay. There are different kinds of videos offered on the auction site, such as how to build a doghouse, how to fix a flat tire and how to cook a turkey. This is a popular one during the holidays.

You can also sell your CD products at places like Café Press and receive a percentage of the profits. These types of physical products are very profitable and people will snatch them up in a heartbeat if it means they can learn more and get more value.

Home study courses are another medium that can be used for physical products. You can have your modified private label rights material compiled in a binder with the pages laminated. Or you can have a combination of a binder and CDs or DVDs as a package set.

Home study courses have a higher perceived value because you have a choice of either reading from the binder or listening and/or looking at the CDs/DVDs. In addition to that, home study courses are very profitable, especially if you created them yourself using modified private label rights.

Master Resell Rights

You can create or have created for you products (e-books, small reports, audio, video or software) made from private label rights and compile them into a bundle. You can offer this package to your mailing list with Master Resell Rights at a special price. This is where you would get you upfront profit.

The subscribers that bought the bundle can then turn around and sell the bundles for profit. It's important that the bundled products are related in one way or another. For instance, if the bundle was about weight loss, then your e-books or reports should reflect that category. These modified products created from private label rights would still have you as the author and would be branded as quality products. Changing the title of the products is important in the branding process.

In addition to helping your subscribers make profits for themselves, you would also increase your mailing list. If the interest is great, you can create volumes using private label rights content. They could be labeled like "Weight Loss Strategies, Volume 1", Weight Loss Strategies, Volume II and so on.

Creating packages like this can present your subscribers with an offer too hard to refuse and will provide plenty of value because the information is not rehashed; instead, you have products that people will want to purchase because of their unique content. They would also value you as an expert and would be willing to buy more from you in the future.

Remember, when you modify these products, it's advantageous to change the graphics and sales letters for more profits. When you create the graphics for your product, use quality graphic software or negotiate with a professional designer. The more professional your presentation is, the more chance you have of people buying.

The sales letter should adhere to your target market. The way to get people to buy from you is to sell them on the benefits—what will it do for me? How is this product going to help me with my problem? How is this product convenient for me? When you provide answers to those questions on your sales pages, you can have profits flowing in like water. In addition to that, you can also include a link to sign up for your list, which can mean a larger list for you, and in turn, more profits.

Bum Marketing

This method is very easy to do and using private label rights material would be a great boost to increase your profits. Bum marketing was based on a concept by a man in Texas who started out with much of nothing and worked his way up making massive profits mostly by article marketing and other methods.

He felt that his strategies were so easy that he could train a bum off the street to do this and he would be making money in no time, hence the phrase "bum marketing". This method is mostly based on writing articles anywhere from 300 to 500 words and submitting them to search engines. You can use private label articles for this because it can save a little time. What you have to do is modify the articles to make them unique and stand out.

When you're writing the articles, be sure to use words that people are familiar with. The more articles you submit, the more traffic you're poised to get. If you kept this going for at least six months on a consistent basis, you could have a nice profit coming in.

The more unique they are, the better chance you have of them getting picked up by search engines. Writing articles is one of the best ways to generate traffic and have profits coming in for years to come. This is because articles that are submitted to article directories stay there and don't get deleted.

In bum marketing, it's better to either have a product created or one you're promoting. If you create a product, you can also use private label rights material to make it unique. Your graphics and sales pages should be unique, also. Or if you want to promote a product, you can check with the marketplace section in Clickbank to get some ideas.

Find out what products are selling in different categories. Check out the sales letter and see how much they offer in commission. If the commission is $10 or more and it's a good product, then you may want to go for it. If it's less than $10, then you may not want to consider it.

In relation to private label rights articles, you'd want to have articles that are related to the product. It's easier if you have private label rights articles that you haven't been using. Search for those on your hard drive and modify them to be submitted to the search engines. The thing about the search engines is they prefer different content as opposed to duplicate content. This works the same way with article directories.

They don't want to have the same articles listed in their database. You want to be able to stand out so that people will notice. Another thing about article directories is you don't want to send the same modified private label rights articles that you submit to one directory to another directory.

You will come out with massive profits if you modify and change the title of the existing private label articles that you have available.

Firesales

This strategy is a great way to tremendously maximize your profit using private label rights content. The content creators use private label rights content to create products. They are packaged in amounts of 10 or more products.

The firesale is constructed as such where the packaged products are sold at different prices for a certain amount of time. For several days, the price may start at $97. After the deadline for that period has passed, the firesale price increases.

The increase could be anywhere from $10 to $30, or maybe more. After that period has passed, the firesale price increases again. This process continues in a cycle for a few weeks or until all the quantities have sold out. With some of the firesales, the prices can increase up to as much as $200 - $250 for a package. This of course, depends on the type of products being sold and how much the seller thinks they're worth.

The products that are sold during the firesale are usually ones that they would rather sell rights to, as opposed to resell the individual products themselves. The seller usually offers private label rights, resale rights and/or master resale rights with the firesale packages.

It doesn't take long for the packages to sell out. For one, there are usually only a limited number of packages made available for the firesale. It's basically a first come, first serve deal. If you snooze, you lose.

The number of packages made available for the firesale are usually between 100 – 300. This way, only so many people are able to purchase. After the last package has been sold, the firesale is over.

They spend several hundred dollars for each product and still come out profitable during the firesale. They don't have a problem doing that because they know they'll come out ahead when everything's said and done.

Just in one day alone, their firesales can amass five figures. Just think, starting the firesale at $97 and 150 purchased at that price during the first few days. That's a total of $14,550 in a matter of 24 – 72 hours. Or sometimes you can make that much selling firesale packages in one day.

If you're thinking about doing a firesale, you can start out with five products. This way, you can get a feel for how a firesale is operated. Some people choose to package related products together, some don't. If possible, see if you can find an experienced person who has done firesales and knows what goes into them.

Take your time to modify the private label content to create your own unique reports. Create graphics to go with them and write your own sales copy. There are many copywriting books available to use. You can also check on the forums. Sometimes, some of the forum members offer great deals on copywriting material. You just never know what kind of gem of a deal you might come across.

Take those five products (or reports) and offer private label rights. Start out with a low price, like $27. Shoot for 50 to 100 packages for your first time. You won't be out of much money, except the merchant processing fees.

If you sold all 100 packages, you could make close to $2600 - $2700, minus the processing fees. Of course, the reports must have excellent value and they don't have to be 70+ pages long to do that. After you've finished the first one, you can do it all over again. You may want to wait a month or two before presenting it. You don't want to get inundated with firesales and lose focus with your subscribers.

Firesales is a surefire way to make a ton of money in a day to a few days. After you really get the hang of it, you can move on to bigger projects that will earn you enormous profits.

One of the best ways to make lucrative profits with private label rights content is to create membership sites. Membership sites can be lucrative because it's considered recurring income that you get every month. It is also a good way of assuring you a consistent online income.

More membership sites are being created all the time. The membership site route will continue to expand. More and more people are looking for ways to make lucrative profits with private label rights content.

By starting out with simple membership sites, you can have a recurring monthly income within 30 – 60 days. Membership sites can be a goldmine, if they're done right. You will receive money every month, as long as your members stick around.

To create a simple membership site can cost less than $50. To set up a membership site may take a few hours, depending on how technically savvy you are. You can find software that can be set up with a few clicks.

Before membership sites became well known, when you installed software, it cost more and was filled with bugs. Also back then, there weren't a lot of merchant systems around to set up monthly billing.

One of the best ways to start a membership site is to purchase bundles of private label rights products and content from sellers and other websites. You can modify the content and use it for your membership sites.

You're just purchasing private label rights content and packaging it for your target audience. When you provide them with private label rights products and content on a consistent basis, they don't have to purchase it.

This way, your subscribers are saving time and money. This also helps your subscribers because they can take the private label rights products and modify them to their specifications.

Before you start your membership site, you should have private label rights content available to upload. You want your subscribers to have products and content to look forward to when they join your membership site. You will have to keep resources available to provide private label rights content to your membership site on an ongoing basis.

A lot of the membership sites out there teach or have information on how to create private label rights products or articles. There are other membership sites that are based on other themes, such as health, recipes, writing and self-improvement, just to name a few. You have to decide on what kind of membership you want to create with private label rights products and content.

When you search for private label rights content for your membership sites, it's crucial to get quality content. If the content is of subpar quality, the subscribers will drop like flies. They don't want to stick around if you have rehashed or outdated material uploaded on your sites.

If you have a problem finding quality private label rights content, you may have to hire writers to create the content for you. You can check with Elance or other freelance writing sites to find people who can fulfill your needs. In order to keep purchasing quality and fresh content, you will have to set aside a portion of your funds for this.

With a private label rights membership site that sells products, you will need to have at least three products available to upload each month. This would also depend on the type of membership and the monthly fee. If you are doing it this way, it would be advantageous to include some private label rights articles to complement the products for that month. This will definitely add value to the existing products.

You can also have a private label rights article membership site. For this, you would probably have to get a dedicated writer just for your site. In order for this type of site to be of value, you will need someone who can churn out private label articles at the snap of a finger. The more articles in the membership site, the better. Some sites have batches of 100 articles or more for that month.

People don't mind paying the monthly membership fee every month as long as you're providing quality content. Depending on the set up, you can charge whatever monthly fee you feel is sufficient to create lucrative, recurring income every month.

Some membership sites just contain private label rights articles and will charge from $10 on up, depending on the content and what else is in the membership site. You can also use another strategy to make quick lucrative income. In addition to offering a monthly fee, you can offer a lifetime membership price where they pay a certain amount one time. They no longer have to concern themselves with a recurring monthly fee.

You can also create membership sites based from niche products that are doing well in sales. For instance, if you have an e-book about vegetarian or organic recipes that is doing well, you can gauge that and turn it into a healthy recipes membership site.

Just fill the site with lots of private label rights articles on being a vegetarian or growing organic foods. People are always looking for subjects like this and are willing to pay money to get these kinds of recipes and other report using private label content.

You can model your membership site after other successful ones. This will give you some ideas as how to tailor your site. You should not, however, under any circumstances, take their work, copy it to your membership site as your own work. You'll be looking at some hefty copyright infringement fines.

You can also conduct niche research to find out what is selling. Clickbank is a great place to start. It is one of the best places to look for and find a niche market to base your membership site on. You can buy private label rights articles on the niche you chose. You can also get ideas for membership sites from bullet points of sales letters. These can provide ideas as to what you can include in your membership site.

Another place where you can get ideas for membership sites is 43 Things. This website is very popular and you can use it to find lots of niche ideas for your membership site. While you're thinking about the theme, you should also think about what kind of problems are people looking to solve. You could probably base your membership site on that, depending on how much private label right content you can get.

Say for instance, the idea was weight loss. The weight loss sector is a popular niche, but if you're able to drill down and find something within the niche of weight loss, like eating healthy, you can create a membership site based on healthy foods/recipes, drinking plenty of water and getting exercise. This all ties in together because in order to stay healthy you must drink plenty of water and exercise.

Amazon is another place where you can get niche ideas for your membership site. Find a niche that catches the eye. You won't run out of niche ideas using this resource. Check out magazines at your local book store. You can find plenty of niche ideas there as well.

When you open your membership site, you may want to have a special for the first 100 people. Some sellers provide bonuses for those early-bird sign-ups. You can start pricing your monthly fees from $4.95. It's better to start on the low end when pricing monthly membership sites because more people are inclined to join.

Even though $4.95 is a low price to start, you can limit your sign-ups to a few hundred. You would make $495 for one site each month. That's a nice little income. Rinse and repeat with the next membership site. You can set it up other small membership sites the same way. You can also have low cost membership sites on: Fishing tips, dating tips, or internet marketing.

There are other ways to find out what people want. You can upload a repot to the membership site and using statistical software, find out how many people read it. When you get your stats, you can look and see which report was downloaded and read the most. This way, you can know what people are purchasing. You can base your findings on that and create products that are related. This way, you're not second guessing what they want.

For your membership sites, it's also good to include small reports. Everyone doesn't like to spend time reading e-books. Small reports can be digested in a matter of an hour or less. As long as the content is of good quality, the subscribers will pick it up in a heartbeat. You can have a few 1,000 word reports uploaded to the membership site. These reports can be created using modified private label content.

You must have a way of getting traffic to your membership site. You can do that by using private label rights articles with a byline at the end. Your articles can be informative, but to the point. Your articles should not have a lot of fluff. You can modify private label articles about getting traffic quickly for your product launch. Modify the articles to your own specifications.

Offer a trial subscription to your membership site. When they go through the site and see what kind of quality content you have created from private label rights material, more than likely, they'll want to stay. People are constantly looking for quality content and they will pay for it!

If you want to create more costly membership sites, you can sell them for at least $97 a month. However, with costlier membership sites, you have to provide more value for what they worth. This means more private label rights articles, private label rights products and other information related to the niche need to be added to the membership site.

To come up with some ideas for your higher priced membership sites, you can use the private label rights reports and articles that come from your lower paying sites. This can generate some ideas as to what niches to use for the higher priced ones.

An untapped way to make lucrative profits from private label rights content is to sell your membership sites for cash. You already have the content modified and created for each site. Membership sites that have original and unique content are winners when it comes to selling them.

This would include e-books, small reports and anything else deemed necessary. The key here, as with private label rights content in general, is uniqueness. Being unique provides value to your membership sites. This means that no one else is creating private label rights content like you.

You have a real winner if your sites are extremely profitable, which is what private label rights content can do for websites. Always create content that has real value and is focused on the subscriber's needs. That's the reason you have the membership sites, for their benefit.

If your site is earning $2,000 each month, you can take 12 months of the profit figures and get a nice five figure sum for selling your membership site. You'd be making a lot more money if you had a lot of these sites. Just do the math.

Just remember this formula: Content that's unique + profitable = lots of money. Your original content can make plenty of money for you, whether it's in a membership site, e-book, small report or videos.

Additional Tips About PLR Content

With your private label rights content, avoid using a lot of pictures and other items that would distract from the narrative. Your customers are looking to receive information, not a lot of pictures.

They can also get in the way and when you try to remove them, it can be a task. It may be better not to have any pictures at all.

When you're writing or modifying your private label content, write it from the angle of the person who you'll be selling it to. They are the ones that will be reading the information, and if it's for their benefit, then by all means gear it towards them. It defeats the purpose if you're not focusing on the needs of your customer. You are there to cater to them.

If your budget allows it and you don't have the time to create private label articles, hire a ghostwriter, check with Elance, or other freelance writing sites. You can get some candidates for a reasonable price. You can also check with the more popular forums to find writers who are looking for writing work. They'll be glad to negotiate a deal with you.

You should have good sales letter copy. It should include the following:

Headline

Your headline is usually in red bold lettering. It stands out because it uses a large font. This is to get the customer's attention. The headline should also be worded whereas it stands out.

It should be something that is attention grabbing the moment people laid eyes on it. It should be something that will force them to keep reading to find out more. You can also have a sub headline. Of course, the sub headline will have a smaller font, but still in bold. It just provides a little emphasis on what's to come.

Sales Page

When your write, write as if you were addressing this to one person. This makes them feel special and privileged that you would send them an offer. You can also list features of your product, but the key is to list the benefits.

What will it do for them? That's what they want to know. If the product does something for them and meets their needs, then more than likely, they'll whip out their credit card and make a purchase. If it doesn't meet there needs or benefit them in any way, they won't even finish reading the sales page.

If this product is a private label rights offer on how to use private label rights, you should pose some potential problems in the sales letter. For instance:

Let them know that you know that there's a problem that needs to be resolved. In this case, the person may be challenged in how to use private label rights. The person may not know how to modify private label content after they've purchased it from a website.

The person may not know how to create a product with the content they've purchased. Knowing how to market unique products may be a challenge. The person is not versed in writing a sales letter. Structuring private label rights articles is out the box. The person needs to know how to create graphics for their product.

Well, since you have a product that can remedy these challenges, you can present it to the person in a way that won't make them feel intimidated or embarrassed about purchasing your product.

Your sales page should answer and solve all their concerns. It should explain how to create a private label rights product step by step. Let the person know that your product explains how to modify private label content and how to create a product with that content.

If they can't write a sales letter, offer suggestions and alternatives. Provide suggestions and instructions regarding creating graphics for the product. If this can be conveyed on the sales page without giving everything away, you will not only have one sale, but many more. There are many people who are not proficient in some of these features.

Assure your potential customer that their needs will be addressed in the product. Also, let your potential customer know of the additional items that will accompany this product.

On your website, provide them the following information:

- What format they will be receiving the product (i.e., PDF, Word document)
- What they can do with the PDF and Word document (i.e., modify content, etc.)
- Modify the content to create different reports you can distribute for free
- Create an e-course with the content
- Create a newsletter with the content
- Sales letter already written (pre-written sales letter)
- Modify the Word document to create articles with a resource box
- Modify and customize graphics to your specifications

On your sales letter, you should include any testimonials if you have them. This makes your product more credible and will prompt your potential customers to purchase the product. Make a special effort to estimate the actual value of your product. This looks good so the potential customer will know how much it could have actually cost as compared to what you're offering.

On the sales page, you should mention that there is a limited quantity of your product available. In other words, you're saying that if you want it, you need to purchase it now. If the person waits later or in a few days, the product may not be available. Limiting copies also holds an advantage for you. This preserves the value of your product.

Software With Private Label Rights

You don't have to know the latest code to create this type of software. You can have a simple program that people can use. It doesn't have to be complicated. The reason for software with private label rights is that if you were to enter into a business transaction agreement with the software proprietor, they would allow you to modify the software to your specifications. You would also able to brand it so that it's tailored to you.

If you had a thought about creating a product from the software, you could do that to appeal to the needs of the market. With private label rights, any changes made can make the software into a great selling product. The profits from this would be more lucrative than just a private label rights project selling e-books.

There will always be a demand for software in the marketplace. There will always be people who will have a need for some type of software, whether it's word processing, spreadsheet, media creation, etc.

You can also get free software from different webpages that offer it. Be sure to read their terms before you settle on what you want. It is important to know that if you're not a software guru, you may want to get an experienced programmer to assist you in looking for any bugs that may be in the software. You don't need to sell any software and the customer is disappointed because bugs are causing it not to work properly.

Terms And Conditions

This section is very important so they'll know what they can and cannot do with the product. It usually includes some of the following:

- Can or cannot be sold
- Can or cannot use in paid memberships
- Can or cannot sell Master Resale Rights/Resale Rights
- Can or cannot sell private label rights
- Can or cannot be given away
- Can or cannot be packaged with another product
- Can or cannot be added as a bonus
- Will or will not offer unlimited private label rights

If you're promoting something like this, it would be advantageous if you had a list. That way, you would be able to offer it to more people and sell more copies to make a maximum profit. Since your subscribers trust you, they wouldn't hesitate to help you make more money. If you have a big list, there's a chance that more people will purchase your product. This is especially true if private label rights products are what they're looking for.

Joint Venture (JV)

Contact other newsletter owners that are similar to your niche and ask if they would like to do a joint venture project with you in regard to profiting from private label rights content. It's better if both parties have a good, responsive mailing list. They would sign up for your affiliate program where they would get at least 50% or more of the sales. This is another way to make profits with private label rights products.

In addition to regular joint ventures, you can employ joint venture brokers. These brokers intercede with referrals of joint venture partners to participate in your affiliate program. They help you to get partners that otherwise, you couldn't get. Of course if since the broker is considered the middleman, they also get a cut of the profits.

OTO or One Time Offer

You can offer what is called an OTO or One Time Offer. On this page, you can present your private label rights product. People do take advantage of these type of offers because they figure it will be their only chance to purchase at a special price, seeing that it is a one time offer.

All of these ideas and components play a key part in whether you are successful in using private label rights content to your advantage for skyrocketing profits.

As you can see from this report, there are many different ways that you can maximize and exceed your profit with private label rights content. If done correctly, you could have a very lucrative and profitable business using private label rights content in no time flat.

www.ingramcontent.com/pod-product-compliance
Lightning Source LLC
Chambersburg PA
CBHW021450170526
45164CB00001B/461